Emergent Publics

Arbeiter Ring Publishing
2-91 Albert Street
Winnipeg, Manitoba
Canada R3B 1G5

Printed in Canada by the workers at Hignell Printing
Cover by Michael Carroll

With assistance of the Manitoba Arts Council/Conseil des Arts du Manitoba.
We acknowledge the support of the Canada Council for the Arts for our
publishing program.

MANITOBA
ARTS COUNCIL

CONSEIL DES ARTS
DU MANITOBA

National Library of Canada Cataloguing in Publication Data

Angus, Ian H. (Ian Henderson), 1949-
    Emergent publics

ISBN 1-894037-13-8

    1. Social movements. 2. Democracy. I. Title.
HM881.A53 2001   303.48'4   C2001-911636-5

emergent publics

An Essay on Social Movements and Democracy

Ian Angus

ARBEITER RING PUBLISHING • WINNIPEG

To my students, in Canada and the United States, who have accepted the intellectual tasks set by social movements, and who will help change the face of democracy in the future, in gratitude for their collaboration.

And to Jery Zaslove and Roman Onufrijchuk, two friends, and two real teachers, who first got me started on this project.

CONTENTS

INTRODUCTION

THIS SHORT BOOK is about democracy understood as a way of life—a cultural practice involving participants' very sense of themselves and their relations to others—rather than as restricted to political institutions. While it argues some specific positions in the context of a coherent theory of democracy, its main task is to introduce the student, citizen or activist to current thinking about democracy. I hope that my readers will be able to take from the book enough understanding to be able to argue with me and to form their own conclusions. As nature abhors a vacuum, democracy abhors experts, especially experts in democracy.

The following chapters propose a theory of democracy by focussing on how public debate is renewed and reformed by social movements. A democratic culture, properly understood, can make a substantive contribution to the moral-political issues that constantly arise, and that have to be addressed by citizens and political thinkers. Democracy, in this basic and far-reaching sense, should perhaps be called *radical* democracy. This underscores the point that genuine democracy is about much more than the institutional arrangements that allow the current consumer capitalist way of life with its attendant inequalities to perpetuate itself. When understood radically, democracy is about the processes of public decision-making to which economic, social and cultural institutions must be subjected in order to be legitimate and binding upon citizens. Such a radical concept of democracy is concerned to *judge* social, economic and political institutions, not presuppose their legitimacy. It is concerned also with how such judgments are made socially and, therefore, with the social movements that propose critical judgments of current institutions and try to persuade others to share them. To call democracy radical in this sense is not to add anything new. Critical participation has been the core of the idea of democracy from its beginning. In our own time, however, there are powerful pressures from large-scale political and economic institutions such as transnational corporations and nation-states that tend to turn "democracy" into a merely formal procedure of approving decisions that have already been made by elites. Against this restrictive and apologetic tendency, to call for radical democracy is to return democracy to its origins in a critique of established power and a concern with how citizens can articulate their needs in order to decide what courses of action to pursue. Democracy is self-government.

Such a radical conception of democracy has come to the fore again recently, after a shift in left-wing political thought that occurred in the final decades of the twentieth century. Left-wing movements and ideas have had a difficult time in recent years in the face of ascendent market-oriented, neoliberal, right-wing politics. This difficulty has led to some major reformulations of the ideas and projects of the Left, a process that is still ongoing. For a generation, the critical energies of activists had been concentrated in social movements such as environmentalism, feminism, gender liberation, city and regional reform movements, national movements, ethnic politics, and so forth. The labour movement maintained a continuing, if somewhat diminished, presence in the Left. These movements, which won some major victories, and addressed some crucial blind spots of traditional Left-wing politics, are likely to continue. But we have also seen an emerging international coalition of these diverse movements protest the dominance of neoliberal economics at international meetings of the World Trade Organization and World Bank. It is, in many ways, a new form of struggle—one that will not leave the diverse movements themselves unaffected. One might suggest that it is characteristic of the emerging coalition that their association for a common goal modifies the movements while, simultaneously, the movements modify the coalition. This is in no sense a return of the "popular front" politics of the 1930s, where "front groups" were used instrumentally by organizations for their own purposes. In retrospect, one might say that a new era of anti-free trade coalition-building began with the rebellion of the Zapatistas (EZLN) in Chiapas, Mexico that announced itself to the world on January 1, 1994, the same moment as the North American Free Trade Agreement (NAFTA) kicked in. It was both a specifically Aboriginal group engaged in identity politics and an inclusive international movement against neoliberal free trade.

These new energies and opportunities correspond to a change in emphasis in left-wing language from class struggle and exploitation to democracy. It is not that there has been an end to class or other forms of domination. But it has become clear that the project of the Left suffered from the absences in this previous language. To regard democracy as the most fundamental term in the political language of the Left is not to deny that there are many forms of oppression and exploitation. Rather, democracy is an ethical and political term that can bridge some of the gaps in left-wing thought and can gather together many forms of resistance into a coalition that asserts the right of every person to participate in making the decisions that affect his or her life.

What absences do I have in mind? The almost exclusive focus on class struggle historically assumed the homogeneity, or basic similarity, of the demands of the working class. In fact, since the Second World War we have seen a plurality of social movements addressing issues of gender, race, nature and political association whose description of different forms of oppression has resulted in many different demands for the end of racism, sexism, domination of nature, top-down decision-making, and so on. Also, both major strands of left-wing political parties— social democratic parliamentary parties and Marxist-Leninist revolutionary parties—oriented themselves to a takeover of the political institutions of the nation-state. In contrast, the new social movements argue that the whole of daily life is political in the sense that it incorporates power and decision-making. For example, environmentalism has shown that our consumer-buying decisions must be considered in relation to industrialism and the way that it treats nature as merely a resource. Feminism has shown how the apparently pre-political realm of the family must, and can be, politicized. The examples could be multiplied. One of the most valuable aspects of contemporary social movements is that they have brought home to many members of the public a much more profound sense of the political than the institutions of the nation-state can ever recognize. This important shift has also influenced the labour movement, which has incorporated many aspects of the demands of the new social movements into their traditional workplace demands—the demand for equal pay for work of equal value, for example. Furthermore, the orientation of the traditional Left toward attaining state power meant that the Left had little critique of the centralizing and anti-democratic tendencies of modern society. Indeed, many of these tendencies were reflected in the rigidly hierarchical and centralized organizational structures of left-wing parties and trade unions. The Left tended to limit its critique to the uses to which state power was put, not the problems created by the centralization of power itself. In this sense, the 1960s was a transitional period in which the rediscovery of participatory democracy existed alongside a homogenizing discourse of anti-imperialism. The conflict between these two legacies of the Left was not apparent at the time because it was still assumed that the working class were a homogeneous group and thus that the critiques of traditional Marxist and social democratic political parties did not entail a simultaneous critique of their practical politics. The politics of everyday life was simultaneously discovered and obscured in the 1960s. Later, this conflict became apparent when the movement was re-absorbed into traditional parties (Marxist or social democratic), on the one hand, and burst forth to create the identity politics of contemporary social movements on the other.

I don't mean to suggest that hierarchical and centralist political parties ever defined the whole of the Left, of course. There were critical currents, the most important of which were anarchism and council communism. The resurfacing of these buried currents gave life to the ideal of participatory democracy in the 1960s. However, the mainstream Left has been, and still is, plagued with certain problems due to its political language and the theoretical assumptions on which its practice was based. To a large extent, we are now at the end of an era and we look hopefully toward the beginning of a new one. Participatory democracy has never been the dominant tendency within the Left; the newness of our own time is that it appears to be the only strain of traditional left-wing thought that is worth remembering and carrying forward. The contemporary turn toward democracy as the fundamental term of an activist, left-wing political language seeks to redress the absences of the past and to hook the various contemporary movements into a coalition based upon an ethical and political vision. The core of this vision is the politicization of everyday life and democracy as a way of life. I hope that this book can play some small part in this great task, and make our understanding of the relationship between contemporary social movements and democracy richer and more complete by considering their historical and theoretical relationship.

* * *

The question of democracy has always been important to active citizens and political thinkers—which should be enough justification for a book. But in recent times democracy has taken a wider role also in philosophical debates, and it might be useful to indicate why the topics taken up in the following chapters have some implications for the philosophical awareness of our time. Significant currents of contemporary philosophy have moved beyond specialist questions and have assumed a role as a hermeneutic, or interpretation, of ways of life. One could distinguish two streams in this transformation. First, there has been a critique of the notion that philosophy should be primarily concerned with the adequacy of descriptive scientific, or knowledge-oriented, discourse. Such scientific representations presuppose, even though they do not discuss, the prior world of experience that is objectified in order to be described by scientific knowledge. This may be acceptable for a special science, but it involves an unacceptable restriction of scope for a philosophical interpretation of a culture, or way of life. The prior, and philosophically more basic question, is how one's experience of the world can be first objectified, in order that it can be later represented within a field of knowledge. From this angle, then, the investigation of the structure and implications of practical experience comes to the fore as a central theme for philosophy.

As a consequence of this shift toward the interpretation of practical experience and ways of life, philosophy has increasingly concentrated on language as the key to understanding practical involvements in the world. Language is not investigated as a special science alongside others, but as a strategy for elucidating the practical world. The diversity of languages, dialects, and vernaculars suggests a diversity of ways of life to be examined and understood. Philosophy thus encounters the problem of "culture" and will eventually be drawn toward a reflection on the plurality of cultures.

Contemporary philosophy finds at the centre of its concerns the moral and political question of engaging in interpretation and evaluation of the multiplicity of ways of life. Reflection of this kind has to confront a serious perplexity: how can one evaluate different ways of life without imposing the criteria of one supposedly preferable form of life on all the others? For, if criteria of evaluation are internal to a way of life, then how could criteria be validly used beyond the confines of that way of life? And, if they cannot, the absence of such trans-cultural criteria leaves issues to be decided by naked power. In the event, philosophy would be able to do no more than shrug in the face of the central ethical and political issues of our time.

In this way, philosophy has rediscovered the question of power, of the political, at the centre of its concerns. To this extent, perhaps philosophy has begun once again to have the meaning that it has for those outside academic institutions. Philosophy takes up the issue of a democratic way of life, which should put it next door to the activists of the anti-neoliberal globalization movement. We must seek to think together these three themes: cultural plurality, power, and moral-political evaluation. This is by no means an easy task, but it is one that is increasingly necessary for those engaged in the social and humanistic sciences to confront. All those who teach know the immediate involvement of youth with the lived dimensions of this knot. Political activists know how it emerges from, and must be addressed by, their actions.

Through democracy understood as a way of life this knot of issues can be confronted. Practically speaking, real, or radical, democracy demands a dismantling of top-down decision-making and the extension of participation in discussion and decision-making to the widest extent possible. Current thinking about democracy must show how its traditional critique of established and concentrated power can avoid an ethnocentrism of moral-political evaluation. One route toward the solution of this problem is in the theory of multiculturalism—a topic which will not be addressed directly in this text. Another is in the theory of public debate and decision. A third focuses on the social movements of our time which bring to public articulation perceived moral-political issues of domination and inequality. This book is concerned with the interaction between the latter two questions: how public debate is renewed and reformed by social movements. The ethical and political components of this knot pose issues both for contemporary philosophy and for a democratic way of life. For these reasons, which are not so much answers as a way of asking questions, we should take very seriously the role of citizen-activists in the way of life that comprises radical democracy. Democracy is not simply about institutional political practices but is rather the core of a style of life—which is perhaps what its deepest impulse has always been.

WHAT IS DEMOCRATIC DEBATE?

EVERY TIME AN ELECTION is called, thousands, even millions, of dollars are spent. Thousands of signs are put up—to be later taken down—and the parties and their leaders dominate the media. There is a great fuss that goes on until the day of the vote, when it stops. A similar ritual takes place regularly in all the countries that we call democratic. All in all, millions of dollars, a huge amount of resources, and a great deal of time and attention are paid to elections. What for? We call other countries non-democratic when they don't have an institutionalized system of elections like ours, but do we ever look closely at why we call this democracy? Is this really democracy? I will suggest that this isn't democracy at all, at least not its most important part.

Democracy means "rule by the people." But if the large

21

body of the people are to rule, and to make important decisions through their representatives, then they need two main things. First, widespread access to relevant information and, second, the ability to formulate the questions that must be decided, that is to say, the ability to decide what is important politically at a given time. These are the key components of a well-functioning democracy. Rule by the people will become, in practice, an oligarchy — which means "rule by the few"— if the majority of the people cannot adequately discuss the pressing questions among themselves before a decision is taken. Consequently, there is a central role for public discussion and debate in maintaining a vibrant and well-functioning democracy.

The democratic institutions that came into being in seventeenth and eighteenth century Europe and America have been very influential in shaping current representative democracy. This applies both to political parties and government institutions, as well as the function of free speech and the press, which is an important component of the public sphere upon which a democracy rests. Institutions give a kind of solidity, a semi-permanence, to social life that usually extends beyond the life of a single person. Thus, they may seem permanent and immovable to individuals. But institutions do change over time, and new institutions come into being. New democratic institutions for public participation and decision-making develop from the meeting places in which as-yet powerless groups exchange their opinions, develop their group identities, and form political agendas.

Democracy is thus a much more dynamic process than a quick look at contemporary institutions may indicate. Established institutions and media of communication must be guarded from control by elites in order to safeguard the process of public debate. To understand the process of democracy, we have to look at the coming-into-being and the passing-away of institutions in relation to the emerging needs of social groups. In later chapters, we will investigate the role of such *emergent publics* and the social movements from which they develop as a way of evaluating the state of contemporary democracy and perhaps anticipating the forms that it may take in the future.

The key role of public debate was recognized early in modern democracies. In 1791 Article 1 of the Constitution of the United States guaranteed that "Congress shall make no law respecting an establishment of religion, or prohibiting the free exercise thereof, or abridging the freedom of speech or of the press; or the right of the people to assemble and to petition the Government for a redress of grievances." At that time, the writers of the Article referred to only two media of communication whereby the public might discuss and debate—in public meetings and through the printed press. This article has been very influential subsequently among other democracies, though it has in some cases needed updating. The Canadian Constitution Act of 1982 used almost exactly the same words, but then went on, after reference to freedom of the press, to add "and other media of communication." Similarly, the 1948 United Nations' Universal Declaration of Human Rights added "through any media and regardless of frontiers."

When people engage in public discussion in order to make decisions concerning their common life, they become, in the real sense of the word, *citizens*. In earlier times, when all important decisions were taken by a king, the people were merely *subjects*—that is to say, they were subject to the law of the land as decided upon by the monarch. But, with the emergence of democracy, the people are not only subject to the law, they also have the power to deliberate and decide what the law will be. Citizens have this double role—they both originate the law and are subject to it—whereas in non-democratic political forms there are not citizens but only subjects. In this way, democracy brings into being a new relationship between people who are engaged in a common activity as citizens.

The common project that citizens share has the important presupposition that, at least in their capacity as civic beings, citizens are equal. They are presumed equal in their right to enter public deliberations and in their capacity to decide. Despite deep differences that may separate citizens in other respects, they must accept each other as equal in this one in order to enter a democratic political order. This brings forth a new identity based on the equality of citizens in a democracy that has widespread implications not only for politics in the narrow sense, but for the mutual self-understanding of citizens in the practice of their everyday lives.

In order for citizens to make informed decisions, they must have access to relevant information. They must have the right to speak and be heard. Therefore, they must have access to public *places* where the give-and-take of discussion allows each citizen to form his or her opinion. By places, I mean literally spaces—such as the marketplace, parks, pubs, street corners, or even living rooms transformed into public places by holding a meeting—but also I mean places in a more metaphorical sense which includes any kind of meeting of minds that allows an interchange. In this extended sense newspapers, pamphlets, and perhaps television, e-mail and the Internet, are also public places. It is these public places, often humble in origin, that have given rise to the democratic institutions, such as parliament and voting, that we normally think of as signs of a democratic society.

From 1791 to 1948 to 1982, and up to today, the issue is the same: the people must have access to meeting places for discussion and debate if democratic rule is to be effective and informed. However, the means for securing this goal change over time. Originally it was primarily a question of public assemblies which the citizens attended in person. Later, newspapers and other print media became important, especially in large democratic states where it was practically impossible for all the citizens to meet together. More recently, television, film, electronic mail and the Internet have become important means of communication which are therefore central to the process of democracy. While the necessity for meeting places continues, the types of meeting places and the manner of guaranteeing unrestricted access to them changes considerably.

One can easily be led astray by thinking that the particular institutions that we enjoy in our democracy—such as secret voting and political parties—are necessary and sufficient aspects of any democracy. They are really simply means toward the goal of securing widespread public participation and may need to be reformed or changed if they no longer meet this goal. The space for public debate and discussion must be effective in relation to the total amount of information and communication that occurs. If it is not, if the public spaces are dwarfed by a constant barrage of non-democratic, non-participatory messages that do not allow for interchange and debate, then it is unlikely that democratic discussion can be really effective. Thus, in order for a democracy to be genuinely effective, it must continually re-evaluate the success with which its meeting places guarantee the integrity and importance of democratic debate.

Social participation requires meeting places—or

sites—where it can occur and *public* participation requires sites in which the give-and-take of discussion and debate are encouraged. We can look across human history, and across many different cultures, to find examples of such institutions for the formation of public opinion. For example, in middle-seventeenth century England the coffee house was introduced and soon became an important institution for the formation of the ideas of the new middle class. In the same period in France, by way of contrast, intellectuals met with the elements of the aristocracy in the *salon*, and it was here that many of the ideas of the French enlightenment were first presented and debated.

In considering a meeting place to be public, the *interchange* of views and their confrontation in argument is crucial to the formation of opinion. Consider, for example, the fact that even authoritarian political regimes use plebiscites in which people are asked to register their preference for a course of action proposed by the government. Even if they engage in this type of consultation, governments may still be anti-democratic. Plebiscites—and also non-government forms of consultation such as surveys or phone-in radio shows—do not have the two key features that a well-functioning democratic public sphere must have. They present the populace with already-defined questions, and thus do not allow the people to determine what are the important political issues for debate. And they consult each person in isolation and do not allow for the changes in opinion that can occur when one enters into the inter-change of views in informed public debate.

The tendency for individuals to be consulted in isola-tion is reinforced by many tendencies of contemporary so-ciety. The prevalence of consumer activities, for example, encourages us to think of the choices we make in an iso-lated manner. When buying tennis shoes at the mall, I do not expect to have to justify my decision to buy or not to buy to anyone else. I do whatever I like without providing any reasons to others for what I do. In the same way, while large crowds often gather for sports spectacles, this does not mean that there is a public process of interchange and formation of opinion at work. There may be 40,000 peo-ple in a sports arena, but they are not directed toward each other in common consultation. They are situated *beside* one another, as it were, watching a spectacle that unfolds in front of them in much the same way that the audience of a film consists of many people attending the same screen-ing, but does not involve any relationship between the audience members. Each one is oriented privately toward the screen. Our society is also characterized by a dramatic increase in marketing and advertising. If I subscribe to a newspaper, a magazine, or a group of some sort, I am put on a list of people with similar characteristics. Such lists are sold to businesses for marketing purposes. It is unlikely that any other society has gathered such detailed informa-tion about its members and the different categories into which they can be divided up. However, each of these activities of gathering and exchange of information deals simply with aggregates—with social groups in which each person is defined through having similar characteristics to the others—none of them have to do with *public* assembly. We live in a highly organized society with many large-scale group activities but very few of these involve the type of interchange upon which democracy rests.

Television is an important factor in this depoliticizing tendency of contemporary society. Most people today get their information about events from television. Television is a mass medium of communication with a larger audience than any previous one. But this large-scale effect does not include any means of entering into debate with the information presented by the television. It does not allow the viewer to ask questions about the material presented. Perhaps most important, there is no way in which the viewer can ask for information on issues that he or she has not heard about. All news is selected and the process of selection itself is invisible, but in the case of television this is combined with an enormous audience such that it has become the sole source of information for most people. Can such an audience be composed of *citizens*? What meeting places could citizens use that might be as influential as television?

For reasons such as this, some commentators have begun to speak of a *decline of the public*. In a somewhat paradoxical manner, our very highly organized society seems to prefer bureaucratic organizations, marketing strategies, and crowd spectacles and entertainments to the cultivation of the reciprocal giving and taking of opinions through the sharing of perspectives and giving of reasons which characterizes the public sphere. Since consumerism, bureaucracy and entertainments often predominate over public discussion, they invade our conception of politics. We begin to think of political life in these terms instead of through the formation of public opinion. This leads to the decline of public life and the rise of social atomization and bureaucracy if we cease to cultivate the necessary skills and relationships that a democratic society requires.

The ancient Greek philosopher Aristotle thought that the ideal size for a city-state was about 2,000 to 3,000 citizens. Enough so that one could know every other person second-hand, one might say. While I would not know everyone else personally, I would know someone who did know that person. When hearing someone speak in a public context, I would know someone who went to school with him, or was her relative or neighbour, and so on. There is good reason to believe that a participatory democracy requires some sort of personal relation between its members, at least at second hand. If this is so, the coexistence of very large-scale organizations with the decline of public life is less of a paradox than it might seem. It is hard for an individual to feel that his or her participation matters to the outcome when an organization is so large that the individual seems, on the one hand, to be like a replaceable cog in a very large mechanism or, on the other hand, an atomized individual who doesn't need to give any account of consumer-like choices to others.

It is of course somewhat idealistic to think that there was a time when democracy functioned perfectly and to describe the bureaucratic and consumerist tendencies of our time as a decline from such a utopian state. It is more realistic to think in terms of two coexisting tendencies. The process of democracy has always had to exert itself against the de-politicizing tendencies of entrenched economic and state power. In this struggle, democratic forces have had a greater or lesser degree of success at different times and places. There are good reasons to be concerned about the current state of representative democracy in capitalist societies. The sheer size of government and corporate bureaucracies, along with the consumer-oriented practices of contemporary capitalism, put practices of democratic participation very much on the defensive.

It is because of such concerns about the depoliticization of contemporary life that some commentators have suggested that we must attempt to discover new ways in which people can participate in the decision-making process of the large organizations that are so influential in contemporary life. They argue that we need middle-range experiences of public life in between the very large nation-state, on one hand, and individual or family life, on the other. Corporations and businesses, government bureaucracies, city and municipal governments—all of these strongly influence our everyday life, yet we do not often expect to have a say in how they operate.

Perhaps if democracy were extended from the official political realm into these other arenas of life an increase in awareness of democratic interchanges would occur. Once a person has a single experience of genuine participation it tends to reverse the tendency to rely on large organizations to provide solutions to perceived problems. The decline of public life might be reversed by such increased forms of participation. If the individual could feel that his or her participation really mattered in some decision-making processes, we might start to expect to have the right to public participation in many, or even all, large organizations. This could also have the consequence of reversing the decline of genuine public participation in established government political institutions as well. For, as is well known, many people do not take advantage of the opportunities that they already have to participate in political life. Before we can expect an increased desire to participate, and a decrease in apathy, people must have the expectation, and the experience, that their participation really matters. They must feel that they can make a difference.

It must be clear, then, that the notion of the public is

an *ethical*, or normative, one. It does not refer to all types of social assembly, but to a specific process of interchange and formation of opinion through the giving and taking of reasons which can function as a *norm* in judging the democratic, or non-democratic, nature of other associations. Public interaction is a precondition, one might say, for the practice of democracy in the sense that its importance is not the same as being in favour of one party versus another, or one outcome versus another of a decision. Neither does public discussion ensure that the decisions made are necessarily the best ones. In even the best-functioning democracy the people might make uninformed, ill-considered or unwise decisions. In that case, they have only themselves to blame. But in general the formation of public opinion tends to lead to better decisions because it doesn't rely only on just one ruler, or a few leaders, but allows many different ideas to be expressed. The process of opinion-formation itself in the give-and-take of discussion and argument provides a corrective against short-sighted or merely self-interested views. For these reasons, the public sphere is a key component of democracy and also a way of determining the degree of democracy that a society has. Democracy is an ideal—that is to say, an idea that can never be perfectly put into practice, but that nevertheless serves us as a way of gauging how well our practice measures up to our ideas. Democracy can be defined as the ideal that all those who are affected by a decision should be able to participate meaningfully in a public interchange that leads to making the decision. To the extent that such public participation is real and effective, we may judge ourselves to live in a functioning democracy.

Democracy has always been a radical idea: the idea that the people can control the functioning of the society, not just its established political institutions, but that people should make decisions about all the issues that affect them. And there is an even more basic point: people should decide which issues are important to them. They should set the agenda. Not the government, not the corporations, not the mass media, but ordinary people should decide what is important and what should be done about it. For this to happen, the public places in which they participate have to have real effectiveness in relation to the other forms of organization and communication in the society.

Participation in public life with other citizens creates a certain form of common experience that can be had in no other way. Citizens are bound together by their belief in the process of sharing, criticizing and modifying their opinions in a continuous give-and-take that, in an important sense, unites them even when they hold different opinions. This form of common experience requires a discourse, a manner of speaking, that also has distinctive characteristics. In this sense we can reformulate the tendency that I mentioned previously, the decline of the public, in a more useful way: as "the loss of civic discourse." And if we are losing a discourse to talk about the importance of public discussion to democracy, we are in danger of losing the essence of democracy itself. In this sense, democracy depends upon a common identity of the citizens, and a common way of speaking in which they express this citizen identity, in order to combat the tendencies toward bureaucracy, consumerism and entertainment that are so strong in contemporary society.

The common identity of citizens in a democracy can be called a *civic identity*—though it must be emphasized that sharing a common civic identity does not mean agreement on all matters of importance. The process of democratic interchange between citizens involves a continuous interplay between what is common, or shared, and what divides them, or in what sense they are different. A common civic identity is crafted through disagreement as much as agreement. The element of contest, of conflict, cannot be removed from politics. After all, we cannot decide to do everything. A decision requires that some proposals be left aside and others accepted. This is the basis for one of the most important aspects of democracy. So important that perhaps we should call it the basis of democratic political *culture*—by which I mean that it is the core of democracy as a way of life and not only as a feature of political institutions. The element of conflict between humans is generic, it runs throughout all human societies.

Conflict has been dealt with by war, by treaty, by violence, by negotiation, by threats and repression, as well as by debate and discussion. While there are many ways of dealing with human conflict, it is the particular genius of democracy to hold conflict within the bounds of civilized social life. The root word of civic life, and civic identity, is the same as that of civilization. Democracy requires a way of life in which the enemy is transformed into an adversary so that differences can be dealt with peaceably and argument can replace violence.

The civilizing task of democracy is to hold human conflicts within the limits of discussion and debate, to craft a common discourse and identity that persists throughout differences of allegiance and opinion. It crafts a culture of respect for the other—for the *differences* of the other, not only what I agree with or share. It is clear enough after the violent conflicts in the world throughout the twentieth century that the democratic solution to human conflict is not applicable under all circumstances. It depends on a common determination to maintain the bounds of mutual respect in social life. The practice of democracy attempts to craft a civic discourse and identity from the shared determination to keep human conflict within civilized bounds.

This book is concerned with democracy as a solution to two interrelated problems: How to give all citizens a voice in the decisions that affect them? And, how to keep the inevitable conflict that will arise between civilized bounds? By examining democracy through the notion of the public sphere, especially modern social movements, I hope to show that democracy is a process going on under our very own eyes. Even today, democracy is as much a *task* as a history—as much about change as stability, and more about the future and the new than a set of institutions or beliefs inherited from the past.

DEMOCRACY HAS ALWAYS
BEEN A RADICAL IDEA

THE DISCUSSION UP to now has focused on the importance
of public debate to democracy. It has argued that the meeting places in which such debate takes place are the core of
the democratic process, that democratic institutions and
practices are developed from these meeting places, and that
the genius of democracy is to replace violence with a peaceful process of argument and negotiation of differences. This
chapter on the breakdown of the postwar consensus inves-
tigates the dynamic of democracy in the contemporary
context of the rise and fall of the welfare state.

After the Second World War, and through the 1950s
and 1960s, society in Western democracies was based on
expanding production and consumption of goods, nearly
full employment, widespread access to education and health
services, a basic level of economic wellbeing guaranteed by

the welfare state and the stability of the institutional forms associated with democracy—such as governments, voting, political parties, and civil rights. Many of these characteristics were lost in the wake of recent trends, which include intensified competition, globalization of the economy, privatization of government services such as education and health, severe cutbacks in social welfare, reduced real wages, an intensified rhythm of work, soaring unemployment and the growth of marginalized groups who are never likely to find stable employment. Beginning in the 1970s, the optimism of the postwar period steadily waned, so that we have arrived at the first years of a new century—and millennium—fully expecting that, for most of us and our children, life will become more, not less difficult in the future, and feeling impotent in the face of the large-scale social and economic forces that have caused this downturn in expectations. A contemporary theory of democracy will have to face this new context squarely and propose new possibilities for democratic action.

One of the primary questions at this point is how the frightened, isolated and competitive individual that is being produced by the decline of the welfare state can recover, or invent, enough commonality with others to initiate social action. How can we recover a sense of community in the present isolated and pessimistic climate? Alongside the increasing pessimism generated by the end of the expanding economy another important social phenomenon has appeared. Social movements have come to influence the expectations of the population. Social movements—such as the environmental movement, feminism, city reform movements, gay and lesbian politics, nationalism and regional autonomy movements—have developed critiques of the ideal of the expanding consumer society that prevailed during the immediate postwar period. While much of contemporary mainstream politics consists of nostalgic dreams of restoring postwar prosperity, or resentments that such a restoration is unlikely, social movements suggest that this "ideal" cannot be recaptured. Nor should it be. They argue that it was built on unsustainable and often unjust practices and instead they propose new directions for future economic and social development. It is through these social movements that some members of the public have come to question the aim of expanding economic, technological and industrial development and have become aware of its destructive environmental and social side-effects. Moreover, it is through social movements that the isolated and competitive individual can be surpassed by an individual sustained and recognized within an active community.

Coincident with the breakdown of the postwar consensus on the welfare state has been the rise of critiques of industrial consumer society by new social movements. In the first chapter I argued that meeting places for debate and discussion were essential if the people as a whole were to set the political agenda and participate in decisions effectively. However, this ideal has never been perfectly fulfilled—even in democratic societies.

If we look back at the origin of public places, it is clear that many people were excluded from participating in them. Greek democracy excluded slaves, women and foreigners from the public assembly. Also, there have often been property qualifications for participating and voting—a practice that was designed to restrict influence on political decision-making to the property-owning elite. Many of our institutions of contemporary democracy have emerged through the social movements that have criticized these exclusions and have fought to extend the franchise. The abolition of the property qualification allowed the working class to enter political life and therefore to bring questions of social welfare (that were not of interest to the well-heeled aristocracy or industrial middle class) onto the agenda of modern democracies. Almost all democracies now accept some responsibility for employment, assuring a minimal level of protection against hunger and poverty, and protection from arbitrary discrimination by employers. Of course, all of these policies are controversial. A large part of contemporary politics involves arguments both for and against such policies. But the fact that these arguments exist at all is a consequence of the emergence of the working class movement into the public arena in the nineteenth century. The new institutions that emerged from the work-

ing class movement—such as unions; socialist, social democratic and Labour political parties; organizations for
public welfare; public libraries; voting by the whole
population; and so on—have become factors to be reck-
oned with in contemporary politics.

Another example of the emergence of a previously
excluded group is the women's suffrage movement that
began in the late nineteenth century and achieved most of
its successes during the twentieth century. A hundred years
ago women were excluded from voting and other forms of
public participation and, as a consequence, they had no
public identity and their concerns had no voice. Today, it is
a matter for open and public controversy whether women
have concerns specific to them, or social issues to which
they are particularly sensitive. As was the case with the
social welfare legislation introduced by the political awak-
ening of the working class, many of the issues raised as a
consequence of women's struggle for the vote are still
controversial. Mandatory child support by fathers,
prohibition of alcohol, support for mothers and children,
battered women's shelters, rape relief and counselling, equal
pay for work of equal value—all these, and many more, are
issues that emerged into politics as a consequence of
women's new political identity. Moreover, there are
women's organizations and institutions that bring these
issues to public notice and thereby affect the agenda that is
addressed in public decision-making.

Through these two examples of social movements that have transformed the issues and institutions of democracy, we can see that democracy—even though it has historically been exclusive and restricted—has enabled social movements to emerge and criticize these exclusions. Thus, there emerges a dynamic of universalization whereby the excluded enter into and transform the content, institutions and concept of democracy. These movements must confront the power and institutions of exclusive democracy. They engage in a power struggle over who will be functioning members included within the democratic polity. However, this is not just a power struggle in the same sense that one might struggle with an aristocracy or an oligarchy. A large part of the struggle for the extension of the democratic franchise is a struggle for entry into public life. This often involves the invention of new forms of community and public participation that eventually become institutions in the enlarged democracy.

The emergence of previously excluded groups onto the political stage not only brings new issues forward for political debate, it also brings forward new institutions and group identities. These new groups have changed the face of politics in modern democratic societies. Nor is this process over. The Civil Rights movement in the United States in the 1950s and 60s brought issues of racial inequality into public debate, as did the international campaign against apartheid in South Africa during the 1980s, which changed radically the perception of the African National Congress and its leader Nelson Mandela. While the South African government tried to portray Mandela as a violent terrorist, the international campaign succeeded in convincing people that he was a popular leader of a social movement and a legitimate fighter for democracy who had been forced to use violent means because of the denial of legitimate democratic means by the Apartheid state. Eventually, Mandela became president of a new South Africa that renounced racism and has made steps toward greater racial and social equality. Out of this social movement emerged a greater consciousness of racism as a factor in international politics, new and transformed institutions in South Africa, as well as in supporting organizations outside it, and a new identity of an international anti-racist movement and a cross-tribal identity in South Africa.

The very content of the politics of contemporary democracies is a consequence of the many struggles against exclusion and for the extension of democracy to more and more citizens. While the idea of political debate and discussion originally began with a rather select group, it has been transformed through centuries of struggle up to the present day into the idea that *all* the people can participate in ruling *themselves* through open processes of discussion, debate and decision-making. Reminding ourselves of this history should make us aware, however, that we cannot merely define ourselves as a democracy and leave it at that. We have to scrutinize contemporary institutions to see if they genuinely encourage widespread participation and we have to be open to the changes that new social movements might propose. Modern democracy has been shaped by the criticism of earlier exclusions and has become increasingly universal through this process of criticism. The idea of democracy should not be discarded because it has often excluded some groups in the past. It should be extended through the creation of new institutions that enlarge the public sphere. This extension of democracy never happens in one fell swoop, and is probably a process that can never be completed as such. Social movements bring new issues onto the stage but they never bring all possible issues or groups onto the stage at once. In this sense, democracy is always an unfinished project. It is an ideal, not a finished state of affairs.

In generalizing public experiences from personal perceptions of injustice, social movements bring new political actors onto the stage of democratic participation that have to be taken into account in subsequent political debates. New spokespeople and leaders, new institutions, and new members of the movement demand to be taken into account in future public debates. It is through these new actors that the basic problem analyzed by the social movement begins to gain a wider influence within the public at large. Now, for example, certain people speak in public discussions as representatives of environmentalists—a group identity that didn't exist (or was very marginal) until recent decades.

Often these new group identities emerge through a process of criticism of their exclusion from the public sphere. For example, women were excluded from coffee houses in England, but they were very influential in organizing the salons in France. In this way, institutional meeting places are defined as much by whom they exclude as by those who are allowed entry. If we look at examples of democratic discussion—such as the Athenian democracy of ancient Greece that has fascinated political thinkers ever since—we find that there was an exclusion of women, slaves, foreigners and children. While the male citizens of Athens enjoyed a greater democratic freedom to participate in the making of public decisions than any others at that time, they denied the same rights to a majority of others in their city. The process of exclusion is an important characteristic of all public spheres that have existed historically. While public opinion may be open and democratic to all those who participate in it, the opportunity to participate itself is often limited and therefore a democracy can simultaneously be quite undemocratic to those whom it excludes from participation. This, then, is another way of gauging how democratic a society is: How extensive, or inclusive, is it in allowing participation in democratic institutions?

Without movements like feminism, the environmental

movement, gay liberation, national liberation, and community development, the institutional trappings of democracy would become just that—an empty ritual at best, a misleading farce at worst. It is these movements that have brought to public attention all of the pressing issues of our time. Political parties and institutions have responded to these noninstitutional cries for change. Often political parties have responded only slowly, and legislative change usually occurs at an almost geological rate. Social movements embody the lively and creative responses of the public to problems that movements define and to which they propose solutions.

Without social movements institutional politics would be even farther behind the times than it is. Therefore, if we want to understand the origin and essence of democracy, we have to look beyond existing institutions to the voluntary and immediate expressions of citizens' needs and fears that emerge in social movements. This is where democracy originates. Institutional practices, such as voting and elections, themselves emerged from social movements in an earlier time. Democracy is a process, not a result. To confuse democracy with institutional arrangements is not only to put the cart before the horse, it is to miss the essence of the process altogether—which is movement and creativity, the desire for change, for inclusion.

Social movements express publicly the discontent of excluded groups and propose changes to address the discontent. This call for unfulfilled social goals that social movements express has a moral dimension. The experience of previous exclusion generates a feeling of injustice—a feeling that a person is being demeaned by his or her exclusion—that is the moral core of contemporary attempts to extend participation in the public sphere. Social movements develop from this sense of injustice and give expression to previously unfulfilled demands in the society. We might say that they express the failures of the institutional structure. In this way, social movements criticize the forms of exclusion that the public sphere used to accept, and propose more inclusive practices and ideas. For this reason, social movements are important to genuine participation in democratic institutions.

It is through social movements that the perceptions of justice that citizens have, and also which unjust social practices should be criticized, are generalized from individual experiences to become public issues and eventually exert an influence on society. Many of the situations from which people suffer tend to isolate individuals within their own private sphere. Such private suffering is certainly unfortunate—and may even be a social injustice—but it cannot be addressed by political action and social policy until it is brought into the open, discussed and recognized to be a situation that affects many people. In other words, until it is defined as a public problem. Social movements perform this activity of making public the private suffer-

ing of individuals and thus make our democracy responsive to new situations.

Social movements push for expansion of the public
sphere by including the previously excluded and by acting
politically within the public sphere to undo, or at least
mitigate, the inequalities that originally kept them out. This
creates a commonality between citizens where none previously existed between citizens and excluded groups.
Politically, slaves and free citizens in Greece, for example,
or workers without the right to organize and factory own-
ers, or women without the vote and male citizens, had very
little in common. Such conflicts have a tendency to
become violent for two reasons. First, because there is no
legitimate channel for protest to occur—so that movements
for change have to disrupt business as usual in order to
express themselves. Second, the privileged and powerful
ones often respond to movements for change with violent
repression. They wish to hold the clock at a standstill in
order to retain their privileges. A public sphere that excludes many from being citizens who can participate in
discussion and decision-making rests on coercion and at
least the potential for violence toward those who are excluded. The expansion of the democratic franchise through
greater inclusion is thus a civilizing influence. By bringing
conflict into the realm of legitimate debate, it tends to
reduce the potential for violence and repression. It creates
a form of interaction that routes previously violent con-

flicts toward public discussion and decision-making.

The taming of conflict that the public sphere—in its best moments—can accomplish allows us to find a point of commonality that unites the different sides of a political conflict. This is the interest in allowing widespread representation of differing views that is essential to democracy. Or, to phrase it more theoretically, it encourages the development of a shared identity of the citizens. The sense of belonging to a democratic political order requires a feeling of commonality with all other citizens in defending and extending the democratic process. Once democracy is underway it tends to extend itself into larger and larger areas of social life. This logic of democracy proceeds through the bringing of greater and greater areas of life into the public sphere through the criticism and reform of previous exclusions. It develops a sense of shared identity among the citizens that entails a conception of universality that overrides, or coexists with, the differences between them.

Universality—or, the group identity of the citizens—should not be understood as something given to us in the past when democratic institutions were set up and that we have simply inherited. It is continually recreated and extended through the social movements that bring new groups and issues into the public sphere. The adversarial conflict to which this gives rise is essential to the extension of participation and the practice of a well-functioning democracy. A better understanding of the *process* of democracy, of how institutions are constructed, criticized and reformed, allows us to see democracy as an ongoing project, as something to which we can contribute in our own time, and also as a goal that is not yet—and perhaps never will be—entirely accomplished. At the very least, it is an idea that allows us to gauge how far we have gone down the road, and to be vigilant for the new forms that democratic participation may take in the future.

We can't take this notion of a common identity of citizens too far. There has been a strong utopian stream of thought in modern democratic politics that supposes that the conflict inherent in political life could be resolved if only the right formula could be found. The neoliberal market agenda, for example, claims that if all social issues were decided by the market then there would be no more social division over what are the right goals to pursue. Similarly, Marxism and some forms of socialism have argued that if the class divisions of society could be overcome, then politics would become little more than administration because there would be no fundamental disagreements over political goals. Even the fascist, Nazi and authoritarian movements of the extreme Right contain this utopian component in their dream of a completely homogeneous nation or people without divisions or internal conflicts.

The utopian dream of an end to conflict over political goals is really a dream of an end to politics itself—the replacement of politics by administration—in which all that would be needed is at most a certain amount of consultation. For example, plebiscites or polls could be used to ask people privately how the goods should be delivered. They would no longer need to deliberate publicly over *which* goods, or goals, the political system should deliver. Thus, the utopian dream of an end to politics attempts to ignore or to suppress the meeting places in which the common goals of citizens are discussed. Whether for fascism, Communism or neoliberalism, the notion of ordinary citizens meeting together to deliberate is a threat. It is this deliberation over the nature of the life we will lead—together, as a society, not as purely private individuals—that constitutes politics and, as such, it necessarily involves conflict over which goals which we ought to pursue. Power is thus an inevitable feature of political, and democratic, life. The element in modern society that would seek to eliminate politics and replace it with administration is a destructive influence in politics. Instead of dreaming of eliminating politics and power, we need to design institutions that can allow political conflict to be tamed and take place in civilized fashion. Otherwise, conflict is likely to spill over and take more destructive forms. Power is not the problem. The problem is the frustration of legitimate means of pursuing the power to implement one's vision of the good life. It is such frustration that leads to violence through exclusion.

Thus, we must not confuse the civilizing effect of public debate with the utopian tendency to believe that conflict can be eliminated entirely. As new political actors engage in public debates, they pinpoint an antagonist— another social group that is pursuing an opposed policy and is responsible for creating the problems which they define. We need to keep in mind that *the public is always divided.* By this I mean that it is in the nature of political life to involve a conflict. One group wants to do one thing; another group attempts to block this thing and do another. Feminism has advocated, and to a large degree succeeded in achieving, access to abortion for women. This is now opposed by anti-abortion groups. Similarly, the achievement of a certain degree of social security by the welfare state is now opposed by a right-wing agenda that is against government spending for social purposes. The successes of environmentalism in influencing public opinion have recently been countered by pro-industry lobby groups and organizations promoting the "wise use" perspective. In public debate one has to take a side, to be for one policy and against another. Each side frames the questions, and sets up the issues, in its own manner and attempts to influence the side that others will take in the conflict.

The expansion of the democratic public sphere through the inclusion of previously excluded groups involves a taming of potentially violent conflict into the adversarial relations of citizens. Although citizens conflict and pursue different goals, such that one side wins and the other loses, citizens share a common identity that persists throughout conflict. This is the source of the civilizing influence that diminishes the potential for violent conflict that exists in all human societies. Social movements remind us that the goal of democracy is peace, but not the rigid peace of the dead, rather the live, peaceful adversarial conflict that is sustained through opposition to injustice and social exclusion.

In the period of economic expansion after the Second World War, there was relatively widespread agreement about the goals of contemporary society—industrial production, consumer society, and social peace. The welfare state contained social injustices and inequalities within a socially acceptable minimum. In recent years, this consensus has fallen apart. The welfare state has been largely dismantled and social and economic inequality is on the rise. Alongside the breakdown of the postwar consensus, social movements have arisen to propose a plurality of goals. The goals of democratic society are again open to c onflict—a conflict that, if we respond appropriately, can be contained within the peaceful adversarial conflict that occurs between citizens.

Social movements have brought new political actors to prominence and influence and have highlighted the moral injuries of exclusion. They have defined our current situation from a variety of perspectives and have thus opened up new alternatives for public discussion. It is with the social movements of our time that the future of democracy rests.

ALWAYS BEGINNING AGAIN

IN THE FIRST chapter we looked at the history and promise of democracy as the setting of the political agenda by the people themselves—rather than any elite or special interest group. This ideal is still a long way from reality, however. The second chapter discussed the universalization dynamic of democracy, especially in the contemporary context of the breakdown of the postwar consensus on the social goals of expanding production and consumption, the welfare state, and stable representative democratic forms. It argued that the new social movements that have emerged alongside this breakdown of consensus are an important contemporary source for the defence and expansion of democracy. This chapter will investigate the process whereby contemporary social movements pose new questions and issues for the public sphere. Through these new issues, conventional ideas are shaken up and new possibilities for defining, and therefore addressing, our situation are discovered. The role of social movements is important in keeping democratic institutions responsive to the population and in extending democratic participation by articulating new issues, developing new institutions and leaders, and inventing new forms of public interaction.

Some commentators question this emphasis. They point out that social movements are relatively powerless in comparison with already established institutions such as private corporations, government or the mass media, who have much greater resources to pursue their agendas. Also, the emphasis on social movements might downplay the plight of the large mass of the population. We certainly must keep in mind that activists in social movements are a minority and that many people have little time to participate due to the stress of work.

Social movements nevertheless have, in the first place, what we might call a *diagnostic* importance—they call attention to the problems of contemporary society, problems that affect many people beyond those who participate in political activism. But even more important, from a long-term perspective, it is social movements that have succeeded in changing institutions and bringing new forms of public participation into being—even despite the great odds they face. Indeed, one of the main questions one should ask about social movements is how they manage to have an influence on public debate and decision-making far beyond their small numbers and in the face of concentrated power.

Social movements are important because they are the form in which the agenda of citizens is made visible to others and expressed politically such that it can be debated and acted upon. Movements are the essence of the *process* of democracy. Institutions like voting and government accountability do not guarantee democracy. They are only the residue of the democratic process, not its heart and certainly not its origin. If democracy means the responsibility of government to the people, its most important component is the expression of the needs, desires and demands of the people. In contemporary society, it is through social movements that democracy is enlivened and extended into new areas. Institutions can't substitute for the social movements that express the unfulfilled needs of the population, craft these needs into a shared point of view, and press for social changes and reforms.

What do we really mean when we refer to social movements? In the first place, the term refers to non-institutionalized social groups who push for a social change of some sort. Movements are distinct from governments, political parties, interest-groups, business groups, and unions, for example, which are supported by existing institutional structures. Second, social movements are distinct from revolutionary organizations because they do not attempt to seize control of the government and change the entire social and economic system root and branch. The main characteristic of social movements is that they focus on a pervasive problem in the present system as it affects a certain group and propose sweeping changes in order to address this problem. They are not single issue groups—like those in favour of tax reform or changes in the liquor laws—and they address the problems of a social group, not just individuals. Feminism, for example, is a diagnosis of the situation of all women in society and proposes certain changes to this situation. It is not just about one issue, such as equal pay for work of equal value, but about a whole range of issues that are based on the basic problem of a pervasive inequality between men and women. Feminism deals with all of the issues related to this inequality because it proposes basic changes in the role of women in society. Similarly, the environmental movement is not just about pollution, or fish, or forestry, or recycling, but claims that all of these issues stem from a basic problem in the relation of human production and economy to nature.

Social movements are critical of systemic features of contemporary society. Thus, they need to withdraw from the opinions and practices that predominate at present in order to develop their criticisms of contemporary society among themselves. To do this, movements create little public spheres internal to themselves and their members that play the same role that public debate plays in the society as a whole. Through an internal public discussion a social movement develops itself into a force that can influence opinion within the larger society. The public spheres internal to social movements develop experiences that had been thought to be merely private or idiosyncratic into criticisms of society shared by a group of activists. The analysis of the "double burden" of work and family arose through such internal discussions in the women's movement. Similarly, the critique of seeing nature exclusively in instrumental terms as a "resource" was made possible by the sharing of other experiences of nature in the environmental movement. These criticisms are refined through discussion and become the common point of identification for the members of the social movement. It is not only a matter of the new opinions and perspectives that are opened up by social movements, but also that the members begin to see themselves in a new way. This is the way that new political actors come to influence the process of public discussion.

This illustrates a further characteristic of the public sphere. The members of a group who engage in discussion and debate tend to develop a certain group identity that distinguishes them from others, such that they are capable of group action in pursuing their policy. Social movements develop alternative forms of identity formation that conflict with the dominant institutions and identities and which therefore interrupt the process of social reproduction and allow the consideration of alternatives. It is for this reason that social movements have an influence that goes far beyond the number of activists directly involved.

Group identities are produced by identification. Identification is a very elastic process. Social movements bring into being new group identities through affecting the process of identification. For example, there have always been women, but only recently has there come into being the social identity of feminists. To be a feminist is to identify in a certain way with being a woman. It is a creative process. Identification can even go beyond other human beings. Many people link themselves to the environmental movement because they identify themselves with nature such that the suffering of a valley, a tree, or an animal is perceived as relevant in the way that the suffering of another human is perceived by most of us as relevant. A group identity is produced by a process of identification whereby an individual person identifies himself or herself with a larger group and its goals. In contemporary society there are groups such as feminists, environmentalists, workers, businesspeople, that act to influence or change public opinion. The boundaries of each group are fluid and difficult to define. Who is a feminist? Who represents the workers? These are very arguable issues, of course. Such group identities come into being and *act* in the public world to influence the course of events. The process of identification creates social groups that criticize and work to transform the status quo.

The deep ecology movement is an example of a movement that has in recent times put itself forward as an actor in situations dealing with the relation between humanity and nature. If social movements produce new actors on the political scene, they also define the situation in which they find themselves and, in so doing, they partially redefine the society in which we all live. This process of redefinition brings to light previously unknown or ignored aspects of society and subjects them to scrutiny and criticism. Industrial societies for decades, and perhaps even centuries, did not ask about their relation to nature. Nature was simply used as a resource to make the consumer goods that are the main justification of industrial society to the population at large. But it was only with the rise of the environmental movement that the use of nature as a resource was questioned. Environmentalists argue that our survival as a species depends upon our being able to see nature as more than a resource—as more than a means to the goals that humans have. The environmental movement thus redefined industrial society in terms of the *exploitation of nature as a resource*, criticized its environmental consequences, and suggested an alternative view of nature.

Deep ecology has brought the relation of human beings to nature in industrial societies into public awareness and debate in an unprecedented way. Deep ecology suggests that nature has an intrinsic value in itself and is not just there for human use. At times it may appear as if they think that humans are necessarily in conflict with nature, but it is really a matter of proportion, and the loss of proportion between humanity and nature in industrial society. Deep ecology's notion that industrial societies exploit nature as a resource without regard for its intrinsic value has come to be widely known, and is often sympathetically regarded, among many people who are not activists within the environmental movement. The public sphere within the environmental movement has not only developed an identity for environmentalists but has allowed the expression of an alternative view of nature that has come to have widespread influence. The redefinition of industrial society in terms of the exploitation of nature for human consumer goods has allowed the general population to express publicly feelings of identification with nature that were previously regarded as irrational or eccentric and thus to discuss and explore alternative attitudes to nature. These prior processes that are initiated by social movements are crucial to the later discussion of specific policy alternatives such as recycling or the granting of fishing licences.

So, social movements bring new actors onto the political stage and redefine the social situation in which they find themselves. They also perform a third task. They define an antagonist, or an opponent, that stands in the way of the realization of their goals. For the environmental movement, industrial society is the antagonist and, more specifically, the social groups—such as business, government and even, to a certain extent, unions—who promote profit and economic growth without concern for its long-term environmental consequences. The goal of economic growth has also been criticized by the alternative technology movement and the community economic development movement. It has also defined an opponent, or antagonist: those groups—such as landowners, investment groups, government and business—that try to control a community from outside. Community development is an attempt to regain control of a community by the members of the community themselves.

By defining its antagonist a social movement clarifies what it is for and what it is against. There are three processes of definition that occur within a social movement: 1] defining itself; 2] redefining the social situation; and 3] defining an antagonist. Through such definitions and redefinitions, social movements shake up the received opinions about what kind of society we live in and what are acceptable forms of behaviour. They make questionable what has previously not been questioned and thereby open up larger areas of social life to public discussion, decision and action. The internal process of discussion within a social movement develops an identity which then comes to influence opinion beyond the movement. The process of defining oneself as a new political actor within a social movement expands the options discussed within the public sphere where decisions are made and thus alters and renews the arena of democratic decision-making.

I do not mean to imply that these processes are successive. They go on simultaneously, and influence each other, even though they may develop unevenly. For example, the contemporary anti-corporate globalization movement has clearly defined its antagonist as the international agencies (such as the WTO, IMF, G8, and so on) that facilitate the removal of community, regional, and national controls over corporate activities and the movement of capital. But the process of self-definition as a movement for radical democracy is still tentative— probably because this movement arose as an alliance of other movements with diverse goals.

If the basic idea of democracy is rule by the people, and if we live in a time in which the meeting places in which this popular rule is exercised tend to be buried under the weight of powerful marketing, consumer, bureaucratic and state organizations, then social movements play a very important role indeed in contemporary democracy. They shake up the received opinions disseminated by large conservative organizations and provide the dynamism whereby the way of life we lead may genuinely be questioned and changed. The public sphere, which we often take for granted in democratic society, originated with the struggles of social movements to get their voices heard. Contemporary democracy relies upon social movements to continue the process of expanding democracy toward the ideal of rule by all the people. Democracy isn't a finished set of institutions. It is just starting. What is important about democracy is always just starting.

I have argued that democracy involves criticism and antagonism. It might sound as if I am courting disaster. We live in a dangerous time in which the possibility that social conflicts may break out into violence is always with us. Social movements bring forth new conflicts because they define actors who criticize mainstream society. They redefine society in ways that emphasize social problems and unresolved issues. And, perhaps most controversially, they define themselves in opposition to an antagonist whose actions are regarded as responsible for social problems. The environmentalist movement, for example, sets itself into opposition with the forces in industry and government who are content to view nature as merely a resource for human use. Feminism sets itself into conflict with those who maintain inequality between men and women. The definition of an antagonist sharpens social conflict. Is not that an invitation to violence? Wouldn't we be better off without such conflicts?

The short answer, I believe, is no. Social conflict and antagonism do not themselves lead to violence. Rather, the suppression of real social issues and unfulfilled needs can lead to violence if no steps are taken to address them. The apparent peace that ensues when all problems are pushed underground is really the sleep of the ignorant. They will be woken when unresolved issues erupt into public life without benefit of the healthy effects of discussion and public interaction. While publics do come into conflict, the role of public discussion is to bring such conflict into the realm of debate where more inclusive solutions can be proposed. Violence does not stem from conflict but from the attempt to suppress conflict. Social movements give us the opportunity to search for solutions.

The interaction between the public spheres and meeting places internal to social movements and the process of democratic debate in society as a whole is the locus of contemporary democracy. Its dynamism stems not from the peace of the complacent, but from the bringing of conflict into the realm of discussion and debate. Conflict is thus tamed, or civilized, into an adversarial relationship and ceases to be a potentially violent conflict with an enemy. Too much emphasis on peace, agreement and consensus leads only to stagnation. Contemporary society often blocks change in the name of consensus with those who have not felt or attempted to appreciate the claims of social movements against institutionalized injustice. One cannot avoid conflict, even though it should avoid being violent and involve a respect for the adversary. It is the blockage of democracy that leads to violence, not its extension.

The public sphere allows us to appreciate the role of conflict in democratic society while keeping the conflict within adversarial terms and not letting it break out into violent form—which seems to be an increasingly common tendency in our time. Only by allowing those people and ideas previously excluded to enter into the public sphere through social movements can the tendency to violence produced by social conflict be checked. It is not by avoiding conflict but by taming it through discussion and debate in the public sphere that democracy advances. Democracy requires the creative energy of social criticism that is carried out by social movements. There must always be the possibility of more criticism, of new and as yet unforeseen movements. Only in this way can democracy be kept alive. The democratic institutions—such as voting, elections, and so on—that we rightly cherish are important not because they guarantee democracy—they don't, and they can't—but because they are the democratic legacy of the social movements of the past. This legacy can only be safeguarded by being open to the social movements of the future.

Indeed, new social movements, working together in new ways, are changing the face of public debate. It is to these *emergent publics* that we now turn.

EMERGENT PUBLICS

THE PREVIOUS CHAPTERS have argued that democracy is more than its institutional trappings. It is the entry of the excluded: process, public debate, definition and redefinition, in which our everyday assumptions are criticized and reformed. Social movements play a key role in this process since they question assumptions and develop alternatives. In this last chapter, I will focus on the role of social movements in developing emergent publics that bring into question the predominant direction of social and economic development and have come to change the face of contemporary democracies. New publics are formed within the internal practices of social movements but then come to influence the public at large.

The feminist movement has long employed a process

of consciousness-raising through the sharing of experiences between women, usually in their homes. In this way the domestic setting was transformed into a centre of democratic creativity. In seventeenth century England, the coffee house functioned in a similar way to involve people excluded from the established political process and to push for democratic reforms. Democratic institutions emerge from the creative activities of social movements—not the other way around—and our democratic institutions, important as they are, cannot safeguard democracy in the sense of widespread participation in decision-making. For that we need the renewed creative energy of social movements.

The ideas developed in social movements eventually come to influence society as a whole. Through this process democracy has engendered a dynamic of universalization and can continue to develop new dimensions in the future. Democracy should not be thought of as an existing state of things but as a process of constantly questioning existing social arrangements by the people that are affected by them. Even the idea of a final resolution in the future is dangerous because it implies that the creative criticism of citizens would not be necessary.

Questioning the assumptions we make in our everyday activities and questioning the predominant relations of power are closely related. Within any society the prevailing relations of power are considered normal by the majority of the population. In order for the system of power to change, something prior must happen. Many people must begin to see these relations of power not as natural and inevitable, but as specific and changeable. That is to say, the common-sense assumption that a relation of power is normal must give way to the notion that it is an imposition, an affront, an injustice, and that it deserves to be changed. For example, in many societies it has been taken for granted that women were lesser than men—that it did not make sense to educate them too much, that they were incapable of being political leaders or skilled workers. Men, and male activities, were seen as the norm and women were judged to be a kind of "deficient man." This assumption, of course, has been attacked by the feminist movement. While women have still not yet achieved equal political power, very few people would say publicly today that women are lesser than men. The changing of the common sense assumption is a crucial part of changing the social relationship of power.

Social movements undertake the process of criticizing the dominant social assumptions. In so doing, they undermine the ideas on which relations of power depend and open up the possibility for the larger population that a change can occur. The question of ideas and assumptions within a social movement might be called the creation of an alternative public sphere or the development of an emergent public. This public questioning of relations of power is emergent insofar as it proposes to change the society as a whole. It is an incipient phase of social change. By putting new questions on the agenda, it opens up new possibilities for political action.

It is by no means easy for new publics to emerge. They must battle for space in the public mind with the established media that disseminate ideas and shape public opinion. The public spheres internal to social movements are almost always very critical of the mass media and its portrayal of them. The corporate ownership of the mass media virtually guarantees that its coverage of social movements will be negative. The task of social movements is to bring forth new and critical redefinitions of contemporary society that are inventive and persuasive enough so that— even in the face of the power of the corporate agenda to influence public opinion—the general public will consider a wider range of options for the future.

A social movement engages in a process of internal discussion and debate in order to share individual experiences and to communicate its perspective to a wider audience of potential activists and sympathizers. It is in these emergent publics that ideas are formed that later may come to have a wider influence. The process of sharing and development of ideas within a social movement requires places where discussion can occur. Sharing of individual experiences, and discussing their larger significance, in such meeting places is the essence of democracy. It is not just that many people are gathered together in the same place as they are in sports arenas, for example. There may not even be many people present. The core of democratic discussion is the exchange of views between individuals and the formation of a common opinion.

Groups that were excluded have often gained entry into the institutionalized public sphere by first constructing their own alternative public sphere. Social movements create their own internal public spheres in which they can develop their criticism of contemporary society, cement themselves into a cohesive and active group, and propose the changes they would like to see. For this reason, it is perhaps more accurate to speak of public spheres in the plural rather than simply the public sphere. The environmental movement, for example, has organizations, meetings, and magazines in which the environmentalist perspective on contemporary society is developed. So does the feminist movement. These public spheres that are internal to social movements act upon, and are acted upon by, the general public sphere dominated by more established institutions of discussion and debate.

The public spheres internal to social movements often develop ideas that later have a wider impact. An idea that is unknown, or considered outrageous, in the society as a whole may be highly influential, or even assumed to be obvious, within a social movement. This process of formation and distribution of ideas internal to a social movement is very different from the influence of established institutions of communication such as the mass media or schools and universities. A very interesting example is a five-page summary of a lecture by Arne Naess called "The Shallow and the Deep: Long-Range Ecology Movements," published in the journal *Inquiry* in 1973. A successful academic philosopher in his native Norway, in 1968 Naess resigned from the university and since has become a worldwide influence on the environmental movement. The term "deep ecology" was used for the first time in this lecture. It has since become commonly used within the ecology movement to refer to the feeling of identification with non-human nature that is the motivation for many activists. While the term has perhaps recently begun to have an impact upon the general public sphere and consciousness, it has long been an important point of reference within the public sphere internal to the ecology movement. An idea developed within the more restricted, internal public of a social movement can come to have a regenerating influence on a much wider public. The circulation of an influential statement within a social movement—like Naess on deep ecology—can have a much larger impact than a long academic treatise or even a popular television show because of its connection with the places in social movements where democratic discussion occurs. Especially in a complex society such as ours, one must be alert to the plurality of public spheres, their different roles and their interactions, in order to understand the process of democracy in its changing character through the publics that will influence its future.

Not only ideas, but also institutions emerge from the internal publics of social movements. Consider the symbolic difference between the adversarial architectural structure of the English-style parliament and the circular structure of U.S. political buildings, for example. English political institutions evolved from the adversarial relation between aristocracy and king and, later, the common people versus the aristocracy. The benches of opposing parties face each other. It is a contest in which one side wins and the other loses. U.S. political buildings, in contrast, are circular. They originate in the Puritan rebellion against the British political system and the utopian attempt to found a new community of equal members. Thus, even though there is more than one political party, and there are opposed policies, the architectural structure indicates that all are really members of a single group. They do not face off against each other, but all face, without distinction, toward a decision-making centre. This symbolic difference is reflected in the less ideological and more pragmatic nature of U.S. political parties.

If we can see the influence of social movements on the ideas and institutions of democracy by looking at the past, we may be able to anticipate future changes by looking at the processes that are currently going on within social movements. Economic decision-making has been, in western capitalist democracies, the prerogative of private corporations and businesses. The effects of these private decisions on the larger community and on the natural environment have been brought to public attention in recent decades by the social movements of our time. As we look at these social movements, we may ask what processes and institutions might allow the community to undertake its own economic decision-making. We may also ask by what means the interests of the natural environment can be brought into political deliberation. We cannot be sure how democracy will change in the future. We can, however, be sure that it must change if it is to properly address the issues that social movements have brought to our attention.

Consider the example of technology. Technology is a major influence on contemporary society and yet assumptions about technology among the public are such that it is generally considered to be beneficial, or inevitable, without being really discussed. The direction of technology is extremely influential for the type of society we have in the future. Yet powerful forces conspire to regard technology as outside the realm of public debate. The social movement known as the appropriate, or alternative technology movement has attempted, with some success, to bring the direction of technological development into public debate. In this way, the assumption that technology has a single line of development has been effectively criticized and rejected. Rather, technology is analyzed in relation to the type of society in which it occurs and what social goals it is designed to promote. The alternative technology movement seeks to influence us to bring the impact of technological development into public debate and to question its goals and purposes.

As pointed out in the previous chapter, a social movement brings a new actor onto the political stage. The alternative technology movement has criticized the large-scale and top-down organization of contemporary technology and argues in favour of a small-scale, more decentralized and participatory notion of technology. It strives to make *the community* an actor in debates concerning economic development and technological change. In fact, the first task for designing an alternative technology is to define who is the relevant community by deciding who is affected by the technology and what are the major ways in which they are affected. The community in its struggle for self-reliance is a key actor for the alternative technology movement. The movement opposes the corporate and state forces that attempt to design communities from outside and to subject them to directives that are not necessarily in their interests. The social movement is thus itself a key force in the emergent public that will define itself as a community by publicly defining its own members and discussing how to pursue its own interests.

While the alternative technology movement began

by addressing problems in the Third World, especially that the form of technological development in advanced industrial societies would not help countries with widespread poverty, it is increasingly applicable to the current state of advanced industrial societies themselves. The reason for this is the breakdown of the postwar consensus that had included support for the welfare state. Inequalities of wealth and power are again on the rise in industrial capitalist societies and it has become very relevant to ask the question: technological development for what goals, and in whose interest? And, an even deeper question, what *type* of technological development?

The alternative technology movement has redefined the system of industrial capitalism in terms of the dependence that it creates for the very large majority of the population who do not make decisions about the direction of technological development. It promotes the idea of the social evaluation of technology and criticizes very strongly the widespread notion that technological development is an automatic and irreversible process. Alternative technology advocates argue that such common sense assumptions concerning technology support the interests of the few who make important decisions about technological development. This is not the same as arguing that technological development is bad. Rather, the alternative technology movement suggests that a certain type of technological development has made communities and individuals more dependent on large corporations and government. It advocates another type of development, one that takes into account the needs and abilities of the whole community. This idea, once developed in small circles and experiments, has become an influential one. Increasingly, many citizens are asking: What type of technology? Development for whom? Who should technology serve? What are the obstacles to a humane development of technology?

Current technological development tends to decrease the amount of labour needed to produce goods, and thus to create unemployment. Some of this unemployment is structural, that is to say, some part of the population will never find employment, due to their lack of education, resources or capital. Meanwhile, as a result of the same process, those who do find work within the capital-intensive, technology-driven workplace are confronted with greater demands than ever. The stress and increased demands placed on those in the workplace build at the same time as the marginalization of those who cannot find a place in it. The questioning of technology that the alternative technology movement has achieved should allow us to see that these two problems are not separate. They have a common origin in a form of technological development that has been severed from service to the community that works or the community in which the industry is situated.

The problem is that productive work has been confused with, and equated with, earning wages. But a great deal of useful work is done in the home, on the farm, or in the streets, all over the place, that doesn't earn wages. If we think of work, and also unemployment and marginalization, in relation to its effects on the whole community, we might begin to re-evaluate this situation. All human energy that is expended in work needs to be regarded from the viewpoint of its useful contribution to human life and community. The goal of this rethinking that is proposed by social movements can be called *sustainable development*. Sustainable development refers to the environmental sustainability of human production, certainly, but it also refers to the sustainability of the human community itself.

Alternative technology is just one aspect of the search for a sustainable community in the emergent publics created by social movements. The breakdown of the welfare state has left individuals alone and feeling impotent when faced by the global power of corporations or governments. In order to break through this sense of isolation and powerlessness, social movements must recreate a sense of community by discussing together what kind of society they want and acting politically to try to create it. Political questions, in this sense, are questions of community—of what we have, or might have, in common—not of our isolated interests or our purely personal woes. Traditionally, civic and public issues have referred to the commonality of humans only, but the environmental movement has made us aware that this can be extended to non-human beings as well. Community involves seeing a common interest in sustaining a shared form of life with other beings, be they human or non-human, who are different. The public consists in creating a common identity that binds together despite differences. To be sure, community is not a simple concept. It is often a task to *discover* who is our relevant community. Also, communities overlap and influence each other. They are often communities in the process of formation, brought about by the shared process of diagnosing a problem and identification with a proposed solution that occurs within a social movement.

Social movements are the crucible for the emergent publics that have altered the face of contemporary politics and are the most important source for the renewal of democracy in the future. Human community and the natural environment are the sustaining basis for individuals and their separate goals. Yet we have concentrated very much on the rights and interests of individuals and very little on their duty to sustain the human and natural community that allows them to grow and prosper. The overriding civic question of our time is how to sustain the nurturing basis for human life and wellbeing. Social movements have turned us toward this larger question and have begun to have an impact on our thinking about how our daily activities might become sustainable in the long term— how our individual activities might sustain and replace the common stock of human and natural ecology instead of drawing from it as if there were no tomorrow.

Obviously, the concept of community refers in the first place to the human community within which the individual lives and works. But I am using it here to refer also to the natural environment that surrounds and sustains human life. The common denominator in these two uses is the idea of *diversity*. It is not only that every human activity is surrounded and supported by other human activities and by nature. It is that these other surrounding activities are of a different type. To do anything one must narrow the focus and concentrate on a single purpose. By concentrating in this way, we become dependent on the web of activities that others perform and that nature achieves on its own. Social movements ask that we change the optic of our vision, that we remember what is common and sustaining behind our single and isolated goals. In our time, it has become crucial to remember and protect the sustaining web of human and natural cooperation between diverse activities and beings.

The creation of community is thus a task, perhaps the main task, that social movements attempt. The ideas that emanate from the internal public spheres and affect the general social process of debate revolve around different possibilities for community that we may act to bring into being. This process requires thought, of course, but it goes beyond rational analysis and is really about the kind of world we want to live in, the kind of world we are willing to try to bring into being. Action requires a decision and a real decision can never be entirely reduced to explanations. It is creative and involves the ability to bring never-before-seen things into the world.

In the tradition of political thinking, the term "public" has referred to that which the human community held in common and the manner in which people deliberated about how to live the common life. Today, social movements are reminding us of the importance of recovering and redesigning the common life and are expanding the scope of those who can participate fully in the human community. Even more, they are going beyond a concern with human community to include the natural environment that sustains humans. The idea of sustainability can perhaps stand as a central idea in this expansion of the idea of community, an idea that reminds us of the centrality of diversity to community. Publics come into conflict, and will continue to do so, because the best route to sustainable human and natural life will always be contested. But in and through this conflict, we attempt to discover that which holds us all together. Conflict occurs within community. And the widest boundaries of our community still remain to be discovered.

This short book has attempted to provide a framework for thinking on the subject of democracy. At present, the established democratic institutions seem remarkably incapable of dealing effectively with the pressing social issues of our time. There is widespread disillusionment, apathy, and a sense of powerlessness. There are also active social movements vying for our attention and pressing for change with a striking vitality. I believe that it is with these movements that the hope for democracy rests. This is not at all a new idea. It is the heritage of previous social movements that we benefit from today. A look at the *process* of democracy, at its capacity to change with the new issues and conflicts that come onto the scene, leaves us with a more hopeful picture. If we look for what is inventive in the social movements of our time, the prospects of democracy look quite good indeed.

FURTHER READING

CHAPTER 1: WHAT IS DEMOCRATIC DEBATE?

The contemporary classic text that addresses the theoretical and historical formation of the public sphere is Jürgen Habermas, *The Structural Transformation of the Public Sphere*, trans. Thomas Burger (MIT Press: Cambridge, 1989). Habermas argues that the bourgeois public sphere that defined a realm of public participation in politics was always tied up with assumptions about the ownership of property that limited both the extent of public participation and the issues that were discussed. These internal limitations have led to the decline of the public sphere in the twentieth century such that both culture and politics tend to be delivered to a passive public rather than generated by public discussion. Habermas, in limiting his discussion to the bourgeois public sphere, leaves aside issues concerning "alternative" public spheres generated by social movements and the expansion of the public sphere due to the gradual extension of the vote to all citizens. The public sphere was gradually expanded by movements of the working class and of women, although the tendency to a decline of its real influence due to property limitations must be considered of equal importance. Democratic capitalist societies should be understood as incorporating a tension between these two tendencies of expansion and restriction of the public sphere.

For readers of German, Habermas' book was immediately confronted by the criticism and extension of his argument into questions of the workers' movement and socialist organization that were influential during the 1960s. A book by Oskar Negt and Alexander Kluge entitled *Public Sphere and Experience: toward an analysis of the bourgeois and proletarian public spheres*, trans. Peter Labanyi, Jamie Daniel and Assenka Oksiloff (Minneapolis: Minnesota University Press, 1993) was the lightening-rod for this debate. This text has also only recently been translated into English.

Although Habermas' book was only published quite recently (1989) in English, it nevertheless has had considerable influence in English-language discussions since its publication in German in 1962. This has been partly due

to other writings of Habermas that have used the conclusions of this book, such as the essays collected in *Toward a
Rational Society*, trans. Jeremy J. Shapiro (Boston: Beacon
Press, 1970), partly due to the influence of an encyclope-
dia article "The Public Sphere" published in *New German
Critique* (No. 3, Fall 1974, pp. 45-87) by Habermas that
summarizes his book, and partly due to the many writers
in English influenced by his work.

Many texts have extended Habermas' argument to
these issues of expansion and restriction such that it has
gained both in historical detail and contemporary relevance.
Two collections in English should be noted: Craig Calhoun
(editor), *Habermas and the Public Sphere* (MIT Press: Cambridge, 1992) and John Forester (editor), *Critical Theory
and Public Life* (MIT Press, Cambridge, 1985). In particular, an essay by Nancy Fraser in the collection edited by
Craig Calhoun argues that there is always a plurality of
competing public spheres and that "subaltern
counterpublics" generated by social movements are important understanding public debate in democratic societies.
This essay brings the discussion initiated by Habermas
much closer to the issues raised by new social movements
and surpasses the earlier discussion initiated by Negt and
Kluge in which it was assumed that there would be one
alternative "proletarian" public sphere.

The connection between democracy and public discussion is now well established and the recent translation

of texts by Habermas and Negt and Kluge encounters a different situation from that in which they were first written. In particular, the perspective of "new social movements" pressing a plurality of demands has surpassed the assumption dominant in the 1960s of a class struggle oriented around a single pole of conflict. This raises issues for the public spheres, forms of socialist organization, and political goals that need to be formulated in new terms.

Democracy thus incorporates assumptions about the social role of processes of communication. This perspective underlies many critical studies of communication, such as Robert A. Hackett and Yuezhi Zhao, *Sustaining Democracy? Journalism and the Politics of Objectivity* (Toronto: Garamond, 1997) and Robert A. Hackett and Richard Gruneau, *The Missing News: Filters and Blind Spots in Canada's Press* (Ottawa: Centre for Policy Alternatives, 2000). In recent years, there has been a great deal of discussion about the implications of new media of communication, such as the Internet, for democracy. Very few of these discussions, however, address how transformations in contemporary processes of communication, and our understanding of communication itself, pose new issues for democracy. Such a debate is still in its beginning stages. One book that does address these issues is Ian Angus, *Primal Scenes of Communication: Communication, Consumerism, Social Movements* (Albany: State University of New York Press, 2000).

The debate that was initiated by Habermas has now gone much further than his original formulation and has come to embrace issues concerning the constraint of news by capitalist ownership and the role of communication in social movements. For this reason, a reflection on the public sphere and its limits is a good starting point for defining some of the issues facing contemporary democracy.

CHAPTER 2: DEMOCRACY HAS ALWAYS BEEN A RADICAL IDEA

The welfare state that achieved a social consensus in the postwar North Atlantic capitalist countries was a combination of both liberal and socialist elements. Beginning from John Stuart Mill's *Autobiography*—which exists in many editions, such as, for example, John Stuart Mill, *Autobiography and other writings*, ed. Jack Stillinger (Boston: Houghton Mifflin, 1969)—some liberals came to accept the socialist argument that individual freedoms were not available to members of the working class suffering from unemployment, poor wages, stringent factory conditions and unequal bargaining power over the price of their labour. L. T. Hobhouse, in his *Liberalism* (Oxford: Oxford University Press, 1964) which was first published in 1911, formalized this tendency to argue that the nation-state needed to intervene in the market to redistribute wealth and provide some social security.

The main founding document of the social democratic idea of "social citizenship" which provided the foundation for the welfare state, was provided by T. H. Marshall in his influential essay "Citizenship and Social Class" which is now collected in *Class, Citizenship and Social Development* (Garden City: Doubleday, 1965). C.B. Macpherson, in "A Political Theory of Property," which is included in *Democratic Theory: Essays in Retrieval* (Oxford: Clarendon Press, 1973), also argued that rights to unemployment insurance, retirement benefits, public education, and so forth were new forms of property that mitigated, without completely transforming, the older Marxist idea that the working class were propertyless. C.B. Macpherson's work is still one of the most important signposts for rethinking the concept of democracy, the individualist assumptions that tie it to capitalism, and its emerging or possible relation to socialism. See, for example, C.B. Macpherson's Massey Lectures of 1965 entitled *The Real World of Democracy* (Toronto: CBC Publications, 1965) and also his *The Life and Times of Liberal Democracy* (Oxford: Oxford University Press, 1977).

The welfare state involved a compromise between a capitalist, market-oriented economy and sphere of production with a quasi-socialist, needs-oriented sphere organized by public bureaucracies under the control of the nation-state. This compromise began to break down with the electoral successes of right-wing, neoliberal (i.e. free market) parties in the 1980s and has continued until the present such that much of the Left has, as a reaction, come to define its goal as the restoration of the welfare state. This consequences of this historic shift have been discussed in Gary Teeple, *Globalization and the Decline of Social Reform* (Toronto: Garamond Press, 1995).

However, the postwar consensus between left-liberals and social democrats on the welfare state incorporated assumptions that make it difficult to see how it could simply be restored. The assumption of a continuously expanding economy has come upon inherent "limits to growth" in the environment. This argument has been made by many commentators too numerous to mention here. Also, feminist critics have pointed out that the assumption of the "family wage" determined the nuclear family as the social norm and confined women to the domestic sphere. See, for this latter point, Nancy Fraser, *Justice Interruptus: Critical Reflections on the 'Postsocialist' Condition* (Routledge: New York and London, 1997).

The social inclusion of the working class (relative, never total, of course) accomplished by the welfare state has occasioned a shift in socialist politics from a rhetoric of "class against class" toward one of "the rights of citizens." The importance of citizen-identity in contemporary politics, and its potential for including differences within a common discourse of rights and needs, has been underlined by Jean Elshtain in her 1993 Massey Lectures, which have been published as *Democracy on Trial* (Toronto: Anansi, 1993). Chantal Mouffe has argued that the commonality of citizen-identity cannot be taken to overcome the agonistic sphere of conflict between different visions of the good life which constitutes politics in *The Return of the Political* (London and New York: Verso, 1993). It remains an important contemporary question to what extent citizen and/or class identities can provide the basis for social solidarity that can address the inequalities and injustices generated by the capitalist economy. One study which focuses on the construction of a citizen identity in Canada and its transformation into a politics of new social movements is Ian Angus, *A Border Within: National Identity, Cultural Plurality and Wilderness* (Montréal and Kingston: McGill-Queen's Press, 1987). A book which considers a similar transition in the Latin American Left is Jorge G. Castañeda, *Utopia Unarmed: The Latin American Left after the Cold War* (New York: Vintage Books, 1994).

CHAPTER 3: ALWAYS BEGINNING AGAIN

The literature on new social movements has grown by leaps and bounds in recent years. The "newness" of such social movements as feminism, anti-racism, gender politics, city reform movements, and so on is sometimes taken to consist in the fact that they aim to reform the capitalist system rather than to replace it through a revolu-

tionary overthrow. Though "reform" is really a too-loaded
word here. Certain environmentalist visions of an earth
not dominated by humans, or feminist visions of a society
after patriarchy, would have to be understood as at least as
"revolutionary"—in the sense of requiring thorough and
far-reaching transformation—as Marxist visions of revolution (some of which seem to require very little change in
the human relation to nature or the relations between sexes
and genders). So, to call new social movements "reformist"
is really to beg all of the questions that need to be addressed and discussed in a contemporary context. It is
perhaps more to the point that new social movements do
not primarily orient themselves to the nation-state as the
locus of political activity—as do both revolutionary Marxism and reformist social democracy. There are many books
that give an overview of approaches to understanding new
social movements. An early book, which is still excellent,
is Daniel A. Foss and Ralph Larkin, *Beyond Revolution: A
New Theory of Social Movements* (South Hadley, Massa-
chusetts: Bergin and Garvey, 1986). Another book, neither better nor worse than many others in the genre, is
Alan Scott, *Ideology and the New Social Movements*
(Routledge: London and New York, 1995).

The best work on the sociology of social movements
develops the claim that movements should be understood
as forms of activity in which the identity of the participants is constructed in a form that initiates new social

conflicts over the basic structures of post-modern, post-industrial, or late-capitalist, society. The classic thinker in this line is the French sociologist Alain Touraine, who has published many books which argue that the new social movements are the new actors that have replaced the working class. However, his work is plagued with a rather nostalgic attempt to find *the* central social movement of our time so that, on the analogy with the Marxist view of the proletariat, he could identify the social agent that can be expected to bring about total social transformation. Touraine's *The Return of the Actor: Social Theory in Postindustrial Society*, trans. Myrna Godzich (Minneapolis: University of Minnesota Press, 1988) is a good, and relatively short, account of his sociology of new social movements.

However, most commentators have accepted the plurality of new social movements as a given that is not likely to be overcome. In fact, the plurality of movements is often taken as one sign of their newness in comparison to Marxism. Another sign is the orientation of new social movements more to cultural, or communication, issues than those of political economy—though this should perhaps be taken more as an emphasis than a dichotomy. An influential sociologist of new social movements whose analysis begins from these factors is Alberto Melucci. See, for example, his *Nomads of the Present*, (Philadelphia: Temple University Press, 1989). One should note also the contrasting work of Klaus Eder, who has argued that the ecology movement is a politics of the middle class—a thesis which has a certain descriptive validity, but fails to get to the depth of issues posed by Touraine and Melucci concerning the contemporary social transformations that render at least partially obsolete these "industrial" categories of class and have engendered new processes of identity-formation. Klaus Eder, *The New Politics of Class: Social Movements and Cultural Dynamics in Advanced Societies* (Newbury Park: Sage, 1993).

An important and influential work that bears a relationship to the "identity-paradigm" of new social movements, but goes well beyond it, is Ernesto Laclau and Chantal Mouffe, *Hegemony and Socialist Strategy* (London and New York: Verso, 1985). Rather than using the focus on the construction of identity as a benchmark to differentiate new social movements from Marxist revolutionary movements, they show how the construction of the identity of the Marxist revolutionary subject was itself a product of Marxist revolutionary activity. Thus, the focus on identity serves not to differentiate Marxism from new social movements as such, but to define a new approach to politics that they call post-Marxism. The construction of political identities in the activities of social movements supplants a 'positivist' notion of society as prior to political engagement. In their theory, politics constitutes social agents at the most basic level. Thus, the difference between the Marxist revolutionary subject and the post-Marxist, radical democratic subject is defined by the replacement of a politics of "class struggle" by a politics of hegemony (a concept derived from Antonio Gramsci), or what might be called a "politics of common sense." The post-Marxist theory of Ernesto Laclau and Chantal Mouffe has been very influential in circles that had been feeling the inadequacies of Marxist theory to contemporary issues. It has been developed further by Ernesto Laclau in *New Reflections on the Revolution of Our Time* (London and New York: Verso, 1990) and in other subsequent writings.

One possible weakness of the work of Ernesto Laclau and Chantal Mouffe is that the construction of identities by political action is not portrayed against the background of the identities constructed, and required, by the dominant capitalist social formation. Marxist critics have generally assumed that this constitutes a deficiency in their "linguistic" paradigm that must be replaced by an empirical focus on class relations—exactly the understanding of class that Laclau and Mouffe have effectively criticized. See, Norman Geras, "Post-Marxism?" in *New Left Review* 163, May-June 1987 and the reply by Laclau and Mouffe in 166, November-December 1987 and also Ellen Meiksins Wood, *The Retreat from Class* (London and New York: Verso, 1986). Rather, one might argue, the background of capitalist identities constructed in the obligatory "political" activities of capitalist society must be investigated also.

One work which places the construction of social identities within new social movements against the background of, and in conflict with, the construction of social identities in consumer society is Ian Angus, *Primal Scenes of Communication: Communication, Consumerism, Social Movements* (Albany: State University of New York Press, 2000).

CHAPTER 4: EMERGENT PUBLICS

A classic text for the emergence of contemporary feminism is Betty Friedan, *The Feminine Mystique* (New York: Norton, reprinted 1983). It still bears reading for its important analysis of how the problem of feminism is "a problem without a name." In fact, this is not just a problem for feminism but is, rather, a problem for all social movements in their initial stages. Social movements emerge by naming and defining *as* problems situations that were previously accepted as natural. Thus, social movements emerge through a "politics of common sense" that problematizes previously held assumptions, assumptions that are often so common-sense that they are invisible to those that hold them. Such assumptions often make invisible the work that is required by institutions but is unrecognized and unrewarded by them. An excellent analysis of how women's work is treated in this way by educational institutions is Dorothy E. Smith, *The Everyday World as Problematic: A Feminist Sociology* (Boston: Northeastern

University Press, 1987). The literature on contemporary feminism has become very large by now. One useful book that gives an idea of how feminism cuts across contemporary theoretical debates is Seyla Benhabib, Judith Butler, Drucilla Cornell and Nancy Fraser, *Feminist Contentions: A Philosophical Exchange* (New York and London: Routledge, 1995).

The literature on deep ecology has also become very large. Arne Naess's journal article in *Inquiry* (mentioned in the text) has been expanded into a book called *Ecology, Community and Lifestyle*, trans. David Rothenberg (Cambridge: Cambridge University Press, 1989). Naess's work is very influential not only among academics but also among environmental activists. For an introduction to his work, see the interview with Arne Naess by Ian Angus called "Free Nature" in *Alternatives Journal*, Vol. 23, No. 3, Summer 1997. For a comprehensive collection that deals with many aspects of deep ecology, see Alan Drengson and Yuichi Inoue (editors), *The Deep Ecology Movement: An Introductory Anthology* (Berkeley: North Atlantic Books, 1995). A debate between Earth First! supporters of deep ecology and the social ecology perspective of Murray Bookchin, is reprinted in Murray Bookchin and Dave Forman, *Defending the Earth* (Montréal: Black Rose Books, 1991).

The alternative, or appropriate, technology movement has produced fewer texts, though it has had some important successes as a practical movement. Its founding text can be considered to be E. F. Schumacher's *Small is Beautiful* (New York: Harper and Row, 1973). A later evaluation of the approach and its applications was undertaken by one of Schumacher's collaborators, George McRobie, in *Small is Possible* (London: Jonathan Cape, 1981). Given the origin of the alternative technology movement in questioning the importation of technologies from advanced capitalist—or, for that matter, state socialist—societies to the "underdeveloped" societies of the "Third World," it is also closely related to work that has questioned the linear, and progressivist, assumptions of "development" and the way that this has been measured by technological "advance." (I have put all of these terms in quotes since they are all held up to scrutiny by the alternative technology movement because they incorporate precisely the sort of questionable assumptions that they want to analyze.) One recent text which critically analyzes the assumptions of the discourse of development is Arturo Escobar, *Encountering Development: The Making and Unmaking of the Third World* (Princeton: Princeton University Press, 1995).

An important text that shows how contemporary social movements have posed questions for moral philosophy, and which develops the outlines of an ethics of respect based in the criticisms of contemporary society by social movements, is Axel Honneth, *The Struggle for Rec-*

ognition: The Moral Grammar of Social Conflicts, trans. Joel Anderson (Cambridge: MIT Press, 1995). The connection between social movements, critical theory of society, and ethical questions has not been adequately investigated and is an important question for contemporary thought. In this connection, see Ian Angus, *(Dis)figurations: Discourse/Critique/Ethics* (London and New York: Verso, 2000).